The Space Needle

Symbol of Seattle

Robert Spector

Documentary Media LLC
Seattle, Washington

The Space Needle: Symbol of Seattle

Published by Documentary Media LLC
3250 41st Avenue SW
Seattle, Washington 98116
(206) 935-9292
email: books@docbooks.com
www.documentarymedia.com

First edition 2002
Second edition 2006
Third edition 2010

Printed in Canada

Author: Robert Spector
Editor: Petyr Beck
Photo editor: Petyr Beck
Copy editors: Judy Gouldthorpe
                 Hillary Self
Designer: Paul Langland
Publisher: Barry Provorse

Contributing photographers:
Larry and Linda Allen, AllensEye Photography
Lara Swimmer, Swimmer Photography

Library of Congress
Control Number: 2002103679

Includes Index and Bibliography

ISBN 0-9719084-0-0   ISBN-13 978-0-9719084-0-6

Table Of Contents

Following page:
Mount Rainier,
Seattle, and
the Space Needle
from Queen
Anne Hill.

It's a structure like no other, an edifice that defines the word "unique." Six hundred and five feet of sweeping architectural and engineering mastery, it rises up from its tripod base to touch the sky and identify a city. When you see the Space Needle, you know you're in Seattle, Washington, USA.

How many buildings in the world can instantly pinpoint their setting? The Eiffel Tower, of course. The Taj Mahal, the Leaning Tower of Pisa. Just a handful, really. In the United States, only the Empire State Building is as identifiable and as closely associated with its city.

In Seattle, the Space Needle is the center of New Year's Eve celebrations, not only for the Pacific Northwest region, but for the entire West Coast of America. Whether you are dining in the elegant restaurant, huddled with tens of thousands of other revelers at the base, or gazing upon it from one of the many view-points around Seattle, the Space Needle and its annual show of fireworks are the official indication that another year has arrived.

The Needle has been host to royalty, including Elvis Presley, the King of Rock 'n' Roll, Prince Philip of Great Britain, the Crown Prince of Norway, and the Shah and Empress of Iran. Presidents Lyndon B. Johnson and Richard M. Nixon, and presidential aspirants Robert F. Kennedy, Nelson Rockefeller, and Adlai Stevenson—even astronauts John Glenn and Neil Armstrong and Soviet cosmonaut Gherman Titov—have been aboard the Space Needle. From the world of show business, the legendary Walt Disney and comedian/actor Danny Kaye, pioneer broadcaster and Washington State native Edward R. Murrow, Michael Douglas, Kelsey Grammer of the

Opposite: It took more than 3,700 tons of high-grade steel to fabricate the above-ground portion of the 605-foot Space Needle in 1962.

9

World's Fair President Joseph Gandy (second couple from left) and his wife, Laurene, guide Walt Disney and his family through the Century 21 site.

TV program *Frasier*, Mike Myers of *Austin Powers*, Demi Moore, Tim Robbins, Paul Reiser, Vanna White of *Wheel of Fortune*, and numerous professional athletes and world-famous musicians have all taken the 43-second elevator ride from the ground level to the top house.

Over the years, the Space Needle has been featured in a number of movies, including *It Happened at the World's Fair*, starring Elvis Presley, *Parallax View*, with Warren Beatty, and *Power*, featuring Richard Gere. The Needle has also made appearances on the TV shows *Frasier*, *Northern Exposure*, *Twin Peaks*, and many others. Larry King has even broadcast his national TV talk show from the tower.

During the Seattle World's Fair of 1962, the 240-seat Space Needle Restaurant served 3,000 meals a day, and the Needle's one-day attendance was just short of 20,000 visitors.

Elvis Presley and Vicky Tu on the Monorail during filming of *It Happened at the World's Fair* in 1962.

Then and now, the restaurant is one of the busiest in the country. Not surprisingly, the restaurant, with its 360-degree view and revolving dining area, has often won the title of "Best Restaurant with a View."

One not-yet-famous diner was Bill Gates. In 1966, as a reward from his pastor for memorizing and flawlessly reciting chapters 5, 6, and 7 of the Gospel of Matthew (better known as the "Sermon on the Mount"), the then-11-year-old Seattle native won a dinner at the Space Needle Restaurant. Fortified by that wonderful meal, young Mr. Gates went on to co-found Microsoft Corporation and become its chairman—and the richest man in America.

The Space Needle has been the setting for virtually everything that life has to offer. There have been innumerable marriage proposals, many weddings, and one birth, the surprise arrival in 1974 of a newborn in the women's room. Tragically, that same year, the first of the three suicides in the history of the Needle also took place.

Its uniqueness makes the Needle the ideal setting for publicity stunts, such as high-wire acts, a goat-milking contest on the Observation Deck, and a Seattle-to-Minneapolis pigeon race. For six months in 1974, Bobby Wooten,

The World's Fair Circus Berlin high-wire act was performed between the roof of Memorial Stadium and a point 376 feet up the Space Needle.

Celebration of special events such as the 1990 Goodwill Games is a long-standing Space Needle tradition.

a Seattle disc jockey, and his wife took up residence in a 1,200-square-foot "apartment" on the Observation Deck. Wooten broadcast his daily show from a control room next to the apartment. The Needle's Space Age design made it a natural for hosting a "skywatch" for flying saucers in 1966, and when Seattle hosted a science-fiction exposition, special lighting effects made the Needle look like a spaceship hovering in the sky.

In the summer of 1974, restaurant patrons noticed a small private plane circling the Needle. Nothing unusual about that, until the plane's door flew open to expose a naked "streaker" flapping his arms and waving his legs. The patrons applauded the antics before resuming their meals. The following year, a couple of local daredevil parachutists made an unauthorized jump from the Observation Deck. Although the pair was arrested, they were later found innocent of the charge of reckless endangerment. But they did give Space Needle management an inspiration for a publicity-generating stunt. On July 30, 1976, a team of four parachutists made a sanctioned jump

A 50-foot-wide King Crab climbed the Needle during National Seafood Week in October of 1986.

from the Observation Deck as part of a Space Needle promotion for Seafair, Seattle's annual midsummer celebration.

In 1988, when two Seattle restaurateurs, Tim Firnstahl and Mick McHugh, decided to divide up the restaurants that comprised their multimillion-dollar dining empire, they settled it with much flair (and accompanying publicity) by a coin toss from the top of the Space Needle.

Over time, the Space Needle has sewn itself into the fabric of Seattle public life. It's such an essential part of the city that a local TV station has installed a remote camera at the top so

that whatever is going on in Seattle can be seen from the "Eye of the Needle." Champion Seattle sports teams, such as the University of Washington Huskies football team, the Seattle Mariners baseball team, and the SuperSonics basketball team, know they have arrived when their logos and congratulatory messages are painted on the white roof of the Needle. In 1995, when the Mariners made their first-ever playoff appearance, the Needle placed an oversized inflatable baseball on the halo surrounding the Observation Deck.

Space Needle recognition of the Mariners' 1995 Western Division victory and the team's first-ever appearance in the American League playoffs.

13

Seattleites love their Space Needle so much, they want to make sure that developers don't destroy the view of their city icon by surrounding it with tall buildings. In 2001, by a near-unanimous vote, the Seattle City Council agreed to protect the views of the Space Needle from 10 public places in the city: Alki Beach Park, Hamilton View Park, and Seacrest Marina Park in West Seattle; Bhy Kracke Park on Upper Queen Anne; Myrtle Edwards Park and the Olympic Sculpture Park on the waterfront; Gas Works Park on Lake Union; Volunteer Park on Capitol Hill; Kerry Park, which is high atop Queen Anne Hill; and not to mention the Seattle Center, where all one has to do to see the Needle is to look straight up in the air.

No wonder the city's Landmarks Preservation Board named the Space Needle an official City of Seattle Landmark on April 21, 1999, its 37th birthday. In its Report on Designation, the Landmarks Preservation Board wrote, "The Space Needle marks a point in history of the City of Seattle and represents American aspirations toward technological prowess. [It] embodies in its form and construction the era's belief in commerce, technology and progress."

Pretty impressive words for a structure that was born on a place mat, lampooned by the press, laughed at by bankers and investors, questioned by the citizenry, and dismissed by city, county, and state governments. That's really where the story of the Space Needle begins.

The Space Needle,
with Legacy Lights
beaming, as
seen from lower
Capitol Hill.

An Idea Is Born

"Victory has a thousand fathers," John F. Kennedy once said, *"but defeat is an orphan."*

If there is a single father of the Space Needle, his name is Edward E. Carlson. In 1955, Eddie Carlson, 44, was vice president of Western International Hotels (the predecessor of today's Westin Hotels) and a genuine mover and shaker in Seattle. That year, Governor Arthur B. Langlie tapped the Tacoma-born Carlson to be chairman of the State of Washington's World Fair Commission, which was assigned to explore the feasibility of having a World's Fair in Seattle in 1959. The Fair would celebrate the 50th anniversary of the 1909 Alaska-Yukon-Pacific Exposition, a cultural and trade fair that was held on the grounds of the University of Washington and attracted 3.7 million patrons in 138 days, including President William Howard Taft and the legendary orator William Jennings Bryan.

Carlson's decision to become chairman of the commission was the beginning of what would turn out to be an eight-year commitment—without salary or expenses—that Carlson described in his autobiography as "public service at its best."

The pragmatic Carlson knew that "common sense would have dictated that Seattle, tucked away in a far corner of the United States, had no reason to undertake an effort of this magnitude." Carlson recalled an Emmett Watson article from the *Seattle Post-Intelligencer* in which Watson quoted a New York publicist as saying, "I always thought of Seattle as a place where the town prostitute has a pull-down bed." Nevertheless, Carlson and his six fellow commissioners were determined. "Let's try and make this happen," said Carlson, "and not concentrate on why it can't be done!"

Opposite:
New Year's Eve
celebration 2001.

The farsighted luminaries of Century 21 learned the benefits of investing in permanent structures from other fairs in history, including the 1909 Alaska-Yukon-Pacific Exposition, which became a major expansion to the University of Washington campus after the fair.

Around this same time, the City of Seattle was analyzing its needs for a civic, cultural, and sports center, and Carlson joined with other private and public officials to find a suitable site. The city and the state embarked on a joint $15 million land-acquisition program, with each contributing $7.5 million from bond issues. "Presto! It was done," Carlson described the state's contribution. "No public hearings, no debate, just a pragmatic legislature at work."

At the same time, the legislature had approved the incorporation of Century 21, Inc., a nonprofit corporation that was to serve as an independent agency for fundraising for the World's Fair from the private sector. It had its own board of directors. In addition to continuing to serve as chairman of the Commission, Carlson assumed the role of president of Century 21. Carlson was soon succeeded by Seattle businessperson Joe Gandy, who

The Seattle skyline (shown in 1929) had been slow to change before Century 21. Shown framed by Mount Rainier is the 1914 Smith Tower, which was the tallest structure west of the Mississippi River until the Space Needle opened in 1962.

agreed to head the nonprofit company. The Commission and Century 21 had the promise of $15 million from the City of Seattle and the State of Washington, but despite the involvement of people like Eddie Carlson and Joe Gandy, they lacked the strong backing of the Seattle business and political establishment, which were proving to be a difficult sell.

Clearly, the Fair needed a catchy hook, a reason for being.

Imagination led to the successful development of the Seattle World's Fair. Shown is the official World's Fair poster.

The Russians Are Coming!

On October 4, 1957, the Soviet Union shocked the world with the launch of the world's first space satellite, *Sputnik*. Suddenly Americans were concerned that the Soviets were winning what would be called the "space race." For Seattle, *Sputnik* proved to be a lucky break. Instantly, the proposed World's Fair had a theme: Space.

Jim Faber, a longtime Seattle newspaper and public relations man who was on the Century 21 staff, arranged a dinner in Washington, D.C., in March of 1958 with 15 distinguished scientists and United States Senator Warren

Magnuson of Washington State to sell them on the scientific value of the Fair. Senator Magnuson soon secured an initial appropriation of $125,000. From then on, he provided the political and public financing clout on the national level.

The exposition billed itself as "America's Space Age World's Fair," with a heavy emphasis on science and life in the 21st century.

Early on, two important planning decisions were made. First, the World's Fair should serve as a catalyst to build a complex of buildings whose post-fair use would benefit the community for generations to come. This differed from World's Fairs in other cities, where planners raised substantial sums of money, acquired large blocks of land, spent several years promoting their extravaganza, built temporary buildings, and at the conclusion of the fair demolished them all. Second, this fair should be a compact, jewel-box exposition like the very successful British Festival on the river Thames immediately after World War II. However, it soon became obvious that such an ambitious fair could not be mounted by 1959, so the date was changed to the spring of 1962.

Century 21 leaders, including (standing from left) Fred Paulsell, Edward Tremper, Robert Collwell, Otto Brandt, Lee Moran, (seated from left) James B. Douglas, Iver Cederwell, Senator Warren Magnuson, and Eddie Carlson, discuss the Space Needle plans.

Eddie Goes to Europe

In the spring of 1959, Eddie and his wife, Nell, took some time off to join friends, the Moffetts, who were traveling in Europe. The two couples met up in Stuttgart, Germany, a prosperous manufacturing center whose roots dated back to the 13th century. The city, which had been partially destroyed during World War II, had been rebuilt with modern architecture that complemented the style of medieval castles.

When a German friend, Margot Colden, found out that they were going to be in Stuttgart for just one night, she insisted, "Then you must have dinner at the TV tower. This is one place you must see."

Stuttgart Tower.

Mrs. Colden was referring to one of the crown jewels of the new Stuttgart—a 350-foot chimney-shaped concrete television tower that included a barrel-shaped superstructure housing a multi-floor restaurant that was perched on the top like a water glass. The restaurant offered diners a spectacular view over the old city and the confluence of the Neckar and Wesenbach Rivers.

After the Carlsons, Moffetts, and Coldens took the elevator to the top and sat down at their table, Eddie had an epiphany: "I looked out over the city and realized suddenly that I had paid money to ride to the top of a tower to have dinner!" Not only that, it was a weekday evening, and the place was full.

Later that night back at his hotel room, Carlson found that the combination of jet lag and the thought of the crowded restaurant on top of the TV tower made sleep difficult. He thought about the other famous towers people paid to ascend—the Empire State, the Eiffel, the Statue of Liberty.

The next morning, alone at breakfast in the Graf Zeppelin Hotel coffee shop, Carlson wondered, Could a tower do this for Seattle? He decided that not only could a tower serve as a symbol for the duration of the Fair, but it could also become a permanent, easily recognizable symbol of its locality.

At the breakfast table, Carlson doodled pictures on a place mat of what he described as a "clumsy slender tower" with a ring around the top. He scribbled below it the words "Space Needle."

Later that day, he replicated the sketch on a postcard of the Stuttgart Tower and mailed it back to Seattle to Ewen C. Dingwall, General Manager of the Fair. Carlson wrote on the back, "Why not something like this for the fair?"

At Carlson's request, Margot Colden collected additional information on the TV tower. Carlson learned that not only was the Stuttgart Tower a money-making restaurant, it was also a profitable antenna site for TV stations. "If we ever do build one of these," Carlson told Mrs. Colden as he left Stuttgart, "you'll have to be there when it opens."

After Stuttgart, Carlson went to Paris. There, as did thousands of tourists before, he stood in line to get to the top of the lofty old Eiffel Tower (984 feet high), with its sweeping view of the river Seine and the city. He reminisced about trips to the top of the Empire State Building (1,472 feet high), the Washington Monument (555 feet), and Tokyo's spectacular television tower (1,082 feet). "Three weeks later, we were back in Seattle," Carlson recalled. "By this time the idea of building a tower as a symbol for the Seattle World's Fair had become an obsession." Ironically, the Fair's General Manager Dingwall never did receive Carlson's postcard.

The first tower to be built for an international exposition was the Eiffel Tower, constructed as the centerpiece of the Paris Exposition in 1889.

Let's Go See Jack Graham

Upon returning home, Carlson made his first call to an old and trusted friend, James Douglas, who was in charge of construction for Century 21. At lunch at a downtown restaurant, Carlson pulled from his pocket one of the postcard photos of the TV tower and said, "Jim, I can't get this thing out of my mind. We've been trying to find a symbol for Century 21 that would attract attention

Seattle skyline from West Seattle's Alki Beach, 2002.

around the world. The Monorail idea is as close as we've come, and it's still 'yes, no, or maybe' on that. But a restaurant like this, way up in the sky, would tie in with our 'man in the space age' theme. It would reflect soaring and aspiration and progress—even flying saucers. And think of the view from up there: the mountain ranges, Puget Sound, the lakes, and Seattle and the fairgrounds below, as a floor show." Douglas immediately caught Carlson's enthusiasm. The next move? Douglas said, "Let's go see Jack Graham."

John "Jack" Graham Jr. was a nationally known Seattle architect who had followed in the footsteps of his father, John Graham Sr., an émigré from England who established an architectural business in Seattle in 1900. The younger Graham graduated from Queen Anne High School, attended the University of Washington, and graduated from the Yale School of Architecture, where he studied under Buckminster Fuller. He spent five years after

graduation in an executive position with Allied
Stores, which owned Seattle's Bon Marche,
among other department stores. Then Graham
opened an office in New York City. After World
War II, he returned to Seattle to take over his
father's architectural firm. John Graham and
Company was best known for designing large
regional shopping centers, including Seattle's
Northgate Mall, which some consider the
nation's first regional mall. Jim Douglas was
responsible for the promotion and construction
of Northgate and knew Graham well.

Graham, who was called "the businessman's
architect," was immediately intrigued by the
idea of a tower. Examining the postcard of the
Stuttgart Tower, he said, "Let's make the
restaurant revolve."

Members of the
John Graham and
Company Space
Needle design
team: from left,
Nate Wilkinson Jr.,
partner; Rod
Kirkwood, partner;
Jim Jackson,
associate; Jack
Graham; and
Manson Bennett,
senior partner.

The idea wasn't as far-fetched as it sounded
because, at that time, the Graham firm had
already designed a revolving restaurant for the
Ala Moana Shopping Center in Honolulu,
Hawaii. In fact, Graham held a patent on the
revolving restaurant, which traveled on tracks
around a stationary center.

"I'll have the boys do some sketches and
work up some estimates on costs," he told
Carlson and Douglas. "It may not be feasible."
Just as important for the cash-starved Century
21 group, Graham added, "I will speculate
with you on the drawings while you see what
you can do on the financing." Graham, too,
was willing to take a chance.

The Space Needle
top house near
completion in
1962.

The Graham firm had already been brainstorming on ideas for the Fair. Two designers, Jim Jackson and Art Edwards, were working on a futuristic aquarium where visitors would walk through transparent tunnels surrounded by swimming fish. Another concept was an elevated restaurant balanced on hundred-foot legs over a fountain-splashed park. After the meeting with Carlson and Douglas, Graham gave Art Edwards a simple instruction: "Let your imagination go."

Graham suggested that Edwards take his idea of the elevated restaurant and "lift it up high."

Edwards designed a balloon-shaped restaurant that was mounted on a shaft and stabilized with cables running from its top to the ground. With the cables gathered in toward the base of the shaft, it appeared as if they were the ropes of a hot-air balloon connected to its basket on the ground. (The cables were primarily for effect.) Graham then reminded Edwards that he needed an outside elevator to convey patrons to the top. Edwards quickly added a spiral gondola ascent around the outside of the cables.

When Carlson and Douglas viewed the design on June 1, 1959, they liked what they saw. There was just one question: "Could you build that?"

"We'll have to study it some more," said Graham. "We'll do some more sketches, of course."

"Keep going," said Carlson. "We'll be back."

They returned often over the following weeks, looking over many variations on the theme, rejecting additional features, such as an aquarium and a planetarium. Edwards discarded the cables and made the restaurant

Let Your Imagination Go

Opposite:
The Space Needle,
2002.

The Graham-proposed disk-shaped revolving restaurant design concept presented prior to the Carlson suggestion to create a tower.

look like a flying saucer on a single high shaft with a TV antenna spire above. What image could be more appropriate for a World's Fair about space?

Graham, as much businessman as artist, continually thought about how to make the tower pay for itself. He asked Edwards to come up with a revolving restaurant on the tower, an exhibit space that could be leased, and a planetarium dome.

The planetarium idea didn't fly, but the revolving restaurant idea stayed in motion. Graham decided to simplify the design by putting a thin space-disk-shaped restaurant, such as the one designed for Ala Moana, high on a slender shaft. Perhaps additional revenue could come from a TV mast on top.

The concept was daring. Artist Earle Duff created a color rendering that set the tower against a black night sky with green and orange and purple spotlights tracing up the grooves of the shaft. The elevators were depicted as glass cages on cables floating guests skyward. A Space Needle.

Carlson and Douglas liked the design but were certain it would cost several million dollars to build—a lot of money in 1959.

The 1959 Art Edwards illustration of cable-tethered restaurant concept.

30

Then there was the question of whether a 300-seat restaurant could defray the costs of construction.

On December 5, 1959, at a meeting at the Olympic Hotel with Washington's Governor Albert Rosellini, Carlson, and Century 21 President Joe Gandy, among others, the design was cheered—as were the financial projections. But excitement soon faded when local TV stations expressed no interest in using the TV antenna.

The Art Edwards restaurant/planetarium concept.

Back to the Drawing Board

It was now May of 1960, less than two years from the target opening date of April 21, 1962. Gandy traveled to Paris, where he successfully convinced the Bureau of International Expositions to grant Seattle the right to host an officially designated World's Fair. He then visited a variety of countries to negotiate government exhibits.

While in Germany, he visited the Stuttgart Tower—both the spire itself and its financial books. Gandy was impressed. The following month, he checked out the Tokyo Tower, which was inspired by the Eiffel Tower. The Tokyo Tower, he was informed by the president of the operating company, had been an excellent investment. Gandy was more convinced that it made economic sense for Seattle to have its own tower. He just didn't know where the money was going to be coming from.

Meanwhile, the Graham staff was reworking the design. But the engineers made the concrete shaft thick and stocky, while making the restaurant insignificant. "It's losing all its elegance," Graham worried.

With staff designers Art Edwards, Jim Jackson, John Ridley, and Nate Wilkinson all busy on other (paid) projects, Graham brought in Victor Steinbrueck, a professor of architecture at the University of Washington. Steinbrueck was shown Art Edwards' first cable-tethered design. He was told by Graham's partner Manson Bennett that the design could work if each of the cables crossed over the middle and pulled to the opposite side. Bennett sketched a "cage" of cables around the central shaft, spreading at bottom and top, narrowing where the cables crossed above the middle of the shaft. Nate Wilkinson showed Steinbrueck a variation in which he surrounded the shaft with straight rods and then gave them a twist so that they all came together at the center. Steinbrueck drafted several dozen variations. Although none were quite right, Graham implored him: "Keep going."

Jim Douglas wanted to get back to the space-age form of the original Needle idea. Through all the succeeding work, nothing had surpassed that first Edwards-Duff design. But that design had major engineering problems which had still not been solved.

Graham insisted that the top house had to be made flatter, "more like a flying saucer," he said, laying a piece of tracing paper over it. He traced the outer form of the narrow-waisted "caged" tower that Steinbrueck had designed, then drew a wide, disk-like saucer on top.

For the meeting set for August 5, 1960, multiple sketches were narrowed mainly to three styles: the crossed cable "cage" with a round chimney shaft inside, the same chimney shaft without the "cage," and new versions of the cruciform shaft. The chimney form, it was feared, would produce sway problems in high winds. This could be solved by the cables, but everyone considered the cables unsightly.

In September 1960 Barbara Bye presented the John Graham and Company "cruciform" shaft design, which by then was called the "Space Needle."

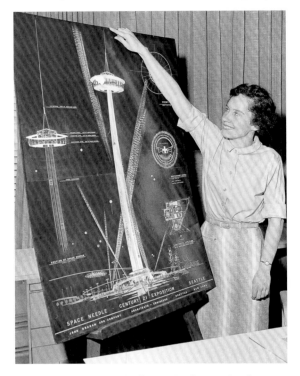

Although the cruciform shaft was back in favor, the Graham research staff felt that customers would be wary of the outside elevators. Graham argued that outside elevators were popular at the El Cortez hotel in San Diego.

The "caged" tower, which was flared at the bottom and top, with a narrow, high waist, seemed as if it could be the basis of a new design. Manson Bennett suggested to Victor Steinbrueck that he give more thought to using a plastic form in concrete instead of cables, referring him to a book by the Italian engineer Pier Luigi Nervi that featured his work with interlaced concrete.

At the same time, Graham designer John Ridley was working on the use of plastic form concrete, which he had been molding into the design of the Ala Moana revolving cocktail lounge. "John Ridley specialized in conceptual design," recalled Rod Kirkwood, an engineer and executive with the Graham firm. "He was very sensitive to intricate detail." Working at his vacation home on Bainbridge Island, across Elliott Bay from Seattle, Ridley tried several different approaches before settling on a shape with a flare at the top and bottom, broadening the curves from a wide bottom to the shaft and back to a wide top with a gradual sweep. Ridley drew a tripod—which could be done in plastic concrete—for stability and support. The following Monday he took his sketches to the office and showed them to Steinbrueck, adding to the burgeoning pile of drawings on Steinbrueck's table.

Early illustration showing the tower set within the World's Fair site.

The Steinbrueck
Space Needle
concept drawing
from the summer
of 1960.

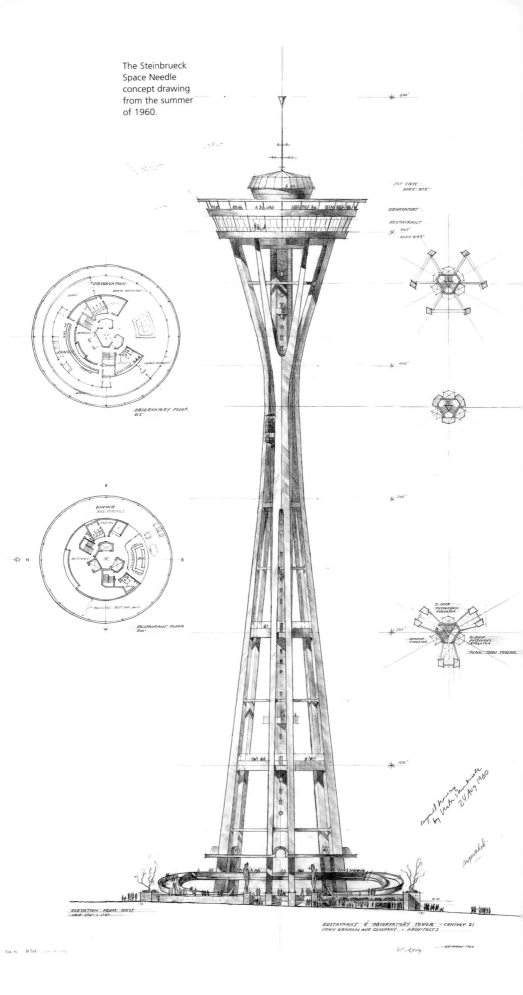

Steinbrueck was also working toward freer plastic form for the cruciform shaft, pinched in at the waist with four legs at the base. When he learned that the planned tower would have three elevators, he redesigned the structure with three legs with elevators between them. After consulting with the other designers, Steinbrueck sketched three outer legs made of two columns, which could presumably be built of hollow box sections of concrete. The three pairs of legs converged at the 370-foot level and then curved out again, dividing into six smaller, equally spaced arms to support the top house ring. Graham liked that part of the design but still wanted to make some changes in the top house. Nevertheless, it was starting to look like what would ultimately be the Space Needle.

The Search for Financing

While the design was coming together, Carlson, Douglas, Gandy, et al. were still faced with one not so insignificant problem: how were they going to pay for it? It was already August 1960.

Carlson decided to make a pitch to King County, the only major government entity that had not taken a financial position in support of the World's Fair. The plan was that the county would supply funds for construction on city land at the Fair, then seek out a responsible

Shown is an early rendering of what would become the Space Needle Restaurant.

Earle Duff rendering of Steinbrueck tripod married to Ridley top house.

private group to lease it for nonprofit operation. Carlson had been looking for a leader for such a group but had thus far come up empty.

In September 1960, Gandy and Jim Douglas, armed with preliminary drawings and a business prospectus, met with the three county commissioners. They proposed building a tower—500 to 550 feet high—crowned with a 220-seat revolving restaurant and an observation platform at an estimated cost of $2,157,000. They contended that the structure, called either the Space Needle or the Seattle Tower, would become a permanent tourist attraction, "a symbol of Seattle," and as such, should be owned by the public rather than a private entity.

The argument wasn't convincing enough. After he received the news from the county commissioners, Gandy headed straight to Graham's offices. "I'm a sick boy, Jack," he said, "but I have to tell you. They turned it down. Two to one."

Graham shook his head and said, "Now that we have the design!"

"I don't care," said an indomitable Gandy. "We're still going to have it, Jack. We've got to have it."

Gandy repeated his commitment publicly to a *Seattle Times* reporter. "Make no mistake about it. Somehow, we are going to have this Space Needle."

Not long after, Jack Graham was in his office with a young, up-and-coming Seattle financier and entrepreneur named Bagley Wright, a former business journalist for the *New York Mirror* newspaper and *Newsweek* magazine who said he got interested in business "as a result of writing about it." At the time, Wright faced a failing deal to build a Graham-designed hotel on Fifth Avenue and Pine Street in downtown Seattle.

"When I was in John Graham's office looking over the design of this hotel, I saw this rather odd-looking 'needle,'" Wright recalled. "On top of it was a replica of the restaurant he had done at the Ala Moana Shopping Center in Honolulu. I said, 'What is that?'"

Graham replied, "That's a project that's never going to get built because the city and the county have turned us down on it. If you want to get some people together to do this, it could work."

Wright was intrigued. He then had a meeting with Joe Gandy, who sold him on the idea. "It sucked me in," he said.

D. E. "Ned" Skinner, who became one of the original Space Needle investors, speaks to city leaders at the dedication ceremony in May 1961.

Wright then met with D. E. "Ned" Skinner, a longtime Seattle businessman and civic leader, who was immediately drawn to the project. As vice president of Century 21, Skinner had been involved in the early fund-raising for the Fair, and Joe Gandy had already shown him the preliminary designs for the Space Needle.

"It makes sense," Skinner told Wright. "Back when we were in school, if you wanted attention, you put up your hand. That is what the Space Needle will do for the Fair and Seattle."

Looking back to those days, Wright said, "Ned and I both looked at it as partially a business opportunity and partly a civic endeavor. Ned had the perfect civic consciousness. He once asked me to join him in buying a part of the Seattle baseball team. I said, 'Ned, I'm not interested in baseball.' He said, 'All the better. You'll do it for the city.' That was Ned."

With Skinner on board, Wright met with Al Link, who managed the real estate ventures of the entrepreneur and builder Norton Clapp, one of the heirs to the Weyerhaeuser fortune. Intrigued but cautious, Link wanted to study the plan more closely.

The idea was solid, but Skinner, Link, and Wright were unready to commit their support to the Space Needle until the plan was better developed. Yet according to Wright, Skinner, and Link, each "was holding in himself a chained enthusiasm."

On a clear day in September 1960, Wright hired the Boeing Company helicopter and invited Skinner to join him in judging the Needle's prospective outlook. They wanted to know how good the view really would be from the restaurant, which was designed to be so high above ground. "We went up 600, 800, 1,000 feet," said Wright. "The view was just

Eddie Carlson, Jim Douglas, and Jack Graham discuss plans for the Space Needle.

as good at 600 feet. . . . In fact, if you go higher, it makes everything look impersonal down there."

Bagley Wright, Ned Skinner, and Al Link agreed to put up the money if they received a guarantee for the loan through a bank. The three investors each owned a 25 percent share in the enterprise. The final 25 percent was split evenly by Jack Graham, who had borne all of the costs to date and was determined to see the project through, and Howard S. Wright (no relation to Bagley Wright) of the Howard S. Wright Construction Company, the then-75-year-old Seattle firm that would build the Needle. In lieu of cash, Graham and Wright each put up the value of their fees.

Word got out, and there was no turning back for the partners. Wright told Skinner, "Well, we have two choices. We can build the damn thing and look up and see what fools we've made of ourselves every day, or we can leave town."

They stayed. The five principals formed the Pentagram Corporation with Bagley Wright as president. Now, all they needed was a site to build a one-of-a-kind structure, which was still being designed, and they had to do it in less than 18 months. The Space Needle group knew that this project would either be the biggest fiasco of their professional careers or the greatest thing they could ever do for the City of Seattle.

Construction company owners Howard H. Wright (second from left), Howard S. Wright (fourth from left), and President of Wright Construction Darby Brown (third from left) inspect the site with steel suppliers.

Following page: The Seattle World's Fair, April 1962.

41

Under the best of circumstances, building the Space Needle would have been a Herculean effort. These were not the best of circumstances.

Consider this. In the fall of 1960 there was less than 18 months to go before the April 21, 1962, opening of the Seattle World's Fair. There was no definite building site. There was no final design. There was no bank loan guarantee. Other than that, it was pretty smooth sailing.

Still, the people behind this project believed in it. They refused to yield to any of the numerous roadblocks that were thrown in their path. That's how the impossible gets done.

"The process was design and plan and finance all at once," recalled Jay Rockey, who headed the Century 21 public relations department. "One didn't follow the other, because there was no time. If you had followed regular procedure, it would have taken a couple of years. Everything was compressed." There was only 18 months left to actually build the Space Needle.

Finding a Site

Where to put the Space Needle within the fairgrounds? The pursuit of the answer to that question ate away valuable months. For a variety of reasons, every proposed site had major drawbacks. Because much of the land on Lower Queen Anne Hill had been acquired by the city by condemnation for use as part of the future Civic Center, there was concern that leasing some of that land to a private, for-profit business might cause legal problems.

With that in mind, the search began for a piece of nearby private land. One possibility was the site of the Nile Temple, which was owned by the Fraternal Order of Masons.

A Race Against Time

Opposite:
Reinforcement steel assembly for the Space Needle's foundation.

Bagley Wright was traveling in Tokyo when he received this wire from his broker: "Smile with Nile. They want a half million dollars." To which Wright wired back, "Nile is a trial. That's much too much."

Wright was prescient. Engineers found that 75 feet under the ground of the Nile parcel was a big storm drain—unsuitable for the foundation of a 605-foot tower.

"You couldn't drive piling to get below the sewer," recalled engineer Rod Kirkwood. "It wasn't feasible in the time we had available. It would have taken four or five months. We didn't have four or five months."

Then there was a service station site across Broad Street from the fairgrounds. It would have been feasible if the builders had received City of Seattle approval for a bridge with an overpass and permission to lower the arterial. The city was amenable, but negotiations with the owner broke down over the price.

It was now January 3, 1961. Al Fast, the Graham project manager, was in a meeting with city officials in the office of City Engineer Roy Morse. "It's a shame," Morse told the city officials. "Are you sure there is no city property anywhere on the Century 21 site that wasn't acquired for Civic Center purposes; something we could sell? Have you searched every title?"

After poring over the deeds for all the property included in the Civic Center grounds, Eureka! Someone discovered a 120-by-120-foot parcel of land that contained switching equipment for the fire and police alarm systems. This property, near the center of the fairgrounds, hadn't been acquired by condemnation because it was already owned by the city, which could sell it to a private venture.

The site was first leveled as part of the city's Denny Regrade project shortly after the turn of the last century, when 140 feet of its crown was removed with steam-shovels and horse-drawn wagons. Graham's soil engineers drilled down 150 feet and found firmly compacted glacial soil that was excellent for the proposed construction, untouched by sanitary or storm sewers. The City of Seattle sold it at a perfunctory auction to Jack Graham for $75,000. Graham bought the parcel in his firm's name because the Space Needle Corporation still hadn't secured a bank mortgage loan.

"We did the soil tests, all the preliminary structural design, and architectural design with no client and nobody paying for it except us. It was done on speculation and on a desire to see this thing happen," recalled Rod Kirkwood. The banks still refused to loan money to build the Needle. "Time was running out, but Graham had kept the design going at our risk. If we hadn't been going ahead all this time and spending our own money up to this point, it would have been impossible to complete in time for the April 1962 opening."

In the early 1900s, the top 140 feet of soil from the Space Needle site had been removed as part of the city's regrade project, which topped hills deemed obstacles to Seattle's development. Shown is the Denny Regrade work in 1907.

Assembling the Pieces of the Puzzle

While the financial institutions were dithering over providing a mortgage loan, they did require that a structural engineer with specific experience in tower design be retained. A logical selection was John Minasian, a consulting engineer and college professor who was a noted expert on towers. In his book on the Fair, the author Murray Morgan described Minasian as "a hulking, beetling, be-mustached expert on tower construction."

On February 10, 1961, soon after the site was acquired, Manson Bennett of John Graham and Company made a phone call to Minasian. "You've been recommended to do the structural design on a tower we're planning up here called the Space Needle," said Bennett. "Can you help us?"

Minasian, who was at his home in Los Angeles grading test papers, had heard of the project and was interested.

"It still isn't financed," Bennett confessed. "We don't know for sure it will go ahead. But if it does, we will need the full engineering by May 1."

"May 1!" said an incredulous Minasian, who knew he'd have to analyze the entire structure before making any major determinations.

A couple of days later, he was in Seattle and agreed to take the job. He would prove to be a key player in this drama, not only for his expertise, but also for his leadership, enthusiasm, and drive.

"The only enemy we have is time," Minasian declared. "I'll fight that with all I've got."

Miss Century 21, Patricia Ann Dzejachok, was an early ambassador of the Seattle World's Fair in 1962.

One Last Attempt

For a variety of reasons, the $4.5 million project was turned down by most of the banks in Seattle, including the National Bank of Commerce (even though both Bagley Wright and Howard H. Wright were directors of the bank). At the same time, a steel erection firm had been expected to participate in the financing, but at the last minute, they bowed out.

"Let's make one last attempt to get the banks to come along," said Al Link, who represented Norton Clapp. On Friday, March 3, Bagley Wright, Link, and Ned Skinner went to see Tom McQuaid, an executive at the Bank of California, Jack Graham's bank. McQuaid was interested. He told the trio that he would seek approval for a loan from the home office and would call them on Monday. First thing Monday morning, March 6, McQuaid phoned to say the loan had been approved. Other banks soon joined in a syndicate to share the financing.

Two days later, the building design received the final okay. Although the Space Needle was originally to be constructed of concrete, Jack Graham made the decision to build the tower of steel because there was too much uncertainty in concrete. A concrete structure would have to be bulky if it was to have adequate strength. The decision to go with steel, which was also recommended by the City of Seattle, added another 30 percent to the price of construction.

"I don't know why we finally decided to go ahead," Wright said. "But the Fair needed it, and there was a lot of civic pressure. We also thought then that we could get a fast tax write-off, which we didn't. I've always been an optimist, and Seattle seemed on the brink of something."

Following page: The Space Needle's continuous concrete pour for the foundation began at 5:00 a.m. and ended 12 hours later. At the time, it was the largest continuous pour ever made in the West.

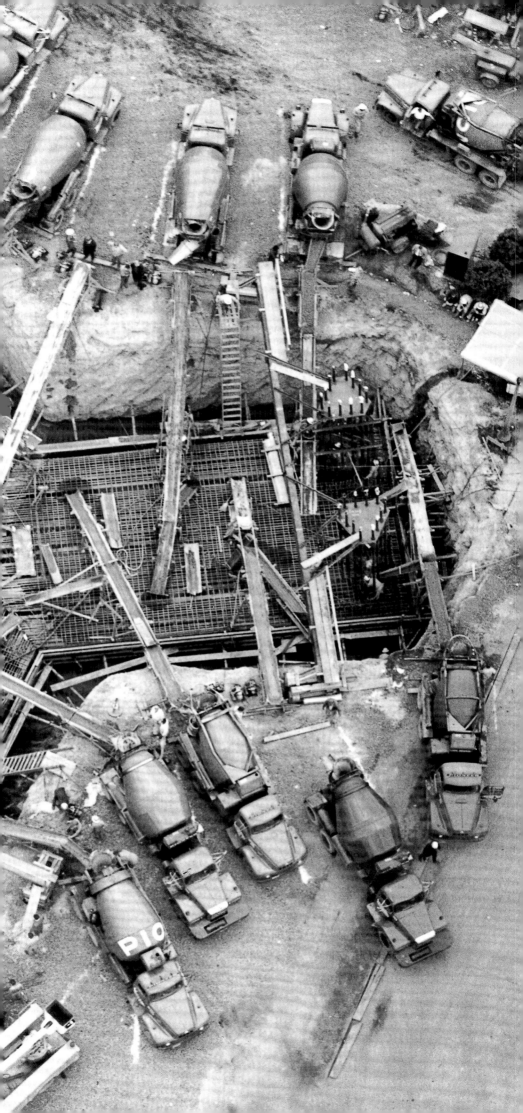

Forms of reinforcing steel were built around four-inch-thick bolts placed as attach points for the Space Needle's fabricated steel legs.

Journey to the Center of Gravity

On April 17, 1961, a year and four days before the scheduled opening of the Fair, the great power shovels of the Howard S. Wright Construction Company trudged onto the grounds and began scooping out the hole for the foundation—a Y-shaped excavation footing, 30 feet deep, laced with 250 tons of reinforcing steel bars. Ninety-six massive anchor bolts had to be precisely placed before the concrete could be poured.

Essential to the engineering of the Space Needle was a low center of gravity. The lower the center of gravity, the more stable the slender tower and its saucer-like top would be.

"We put enough concrete foundation under it so that—if you discount the dirt that's underneath it—the center of gravity is a few feet above ground—not too much more above ground than the top of your head," said Rod Kirkwood. "So the possibility of tipping it over is pretty remote. That was part of the reason for pouring all that concrete; part of it was to make sure there wasn't any deflection in the foundation. If we'd deflected one leg more than another, we would have had the 'leaning tower of Seattle.'"

The pouring of the concrete was quite a show. At 5:00 in the morning on May 26, 1961—less than 11 months from opening day—Harleigh Farwell, superintendent at the Howard Wright construction shack, signaled the first trucks to come rolling in.

They kept rolling and rolling, six or eight trucks at a time. By 5:00 in the afternoon, 12 hours later, 467 truckloads had poured into the foundation 5,600 tons of concrete—enough to fill seven five-room houses from floor to ceiling. It was called the largest continuous pour of concrete in the history of the West. The foundation concrete was a counterbalance to the 3,700 tons of steel in the tower.

For Jay Rockey, who was handling the public relations, "It was a slam dunk to get the local media to cover it." Seattle was finally starting to get excited about the Needle and the World's Fair. National media still viewed the Fair with skepticism.

Among the dignitaries there that day was a gratified and humbled Eddie Carlson, who would later recall, "Watching the pour, I cried a little."

The first of what would be 467 truckloads of concrete was poured into the Space Needle foundation on May 26, 1961.

Going Up

The 90-foot long, 27,000-pound steel beams were shipped from Chicago to Seattle on 65-foot open-end gondolas with flatcars at either end, which acted as "idlers" to permit coupling onto the train.

To achieve the curve at the 373-foot midsection of the leg, it was necessary to weld together three 35-inch-wide "I" beams that weighed 300 pounds per running foot. The beams, which were cast straight, were carefully and precisely curved by Bob LeBlanc's crackerjack crew at Pacific Car and Foundry's (now PACCAR Inc.) Structural Steel Division in Seattle. LeBlanc devised a method of heating pie-shaped portions of the beams.

The first steel leg was bolted to its foundation in June 1961. By November, the top house was already under construction. The rising structure reflected Seattle's rising interest in the World's Fair.

As they cooled, the wide part of the heated section would shrink more than the narrower part, thus curving the beam. LeBlanc described the method as "templates, touch, and horse sense."

The project was submitted to Pacific Car and Foundry as little more than a drawing on the back of an envelope. Preliminary cost estimates were made on a tonnage basis, with only the roughest idea of the form the finished building would take. Justifiably, the steel-fabricating crew had been skeptical that the pieces would fit, but shop superintendent Bob Hermon was confident. "You compute them, and I'll bend them," he told LeBlanc. That was the Space Needle spirit.

With the major engineering problems solved, the first steel leg was lowered onto the giant anchor bolts and attached with equally massive nuts in June 1961. It was straight to the sky from there.

There were many challenges along the way, including one critical one: How would the structure continue to grow skyward once it got above the reach of the crane lifting the first steel sections into place? Paul Collop, the erection superintendent from Pacific Car and Foundry, solved that problem by designing a space crane that fit inside the central tower. The derrick crane literally climbed its way up the inside of the Needle's core. It unfolded its boom, reached out, and hoisted 50-foot, 90,000-pound sections of the tower that the

welders and ironworkers fastened. Then the derrick hoisted itself up the completed section 50 feet at a time.

Collop was a key figure in the construction. The Pacific Car and Foundry boss wrote a weekly column on the progress of the Needle for *The Seattle Times*, and he was also a coach for his crew. "Do it as a team," he told them. "Look out for your buddy. We want no accidents." Collop's words were heeded. No life was lost in the construction.

As the Space Needle rose, so did Seattle's level of interest in the World's Fair. In fact, the construction marked a turning point. "As those giant steel beams went up into the air, it was like a massive Community Chest thermometer rising," recalled Jay Rockey.

"As the Space Needle went up into the air, the intensity of our ticket sales went up with it. This was a big project. It wasn't just building a building, it was building a structure that hadn't been done like this before. By the time the steel got to the top, we were really in gear. We knew then that we were going to make it."

As Eddie Carlson remarked to a friend, "Plenty of people thought we had been selling pie-in-the-sky. And then one day they looked up, and there this thing was, spinning around."

Top of the Needle

It wasn't quite spinning around yet. Except for the elevators, the last piece to be added, in November 1961, was the top house, which contained the revolving restaurant. The disk-like structure was a five-story building: restaurant, mezzanine, Observation Deck, mechanical equipment room, and elevator machine room. Above the steel sunburst at the base of the top house, designer John Ridley created a larger "halo" disk of open structure to shade the restaurant windows and give an outward pattern to the footing of the observation promenade. A gas torch tower topped off the pagoda-style roof.

Top house design cutaway.

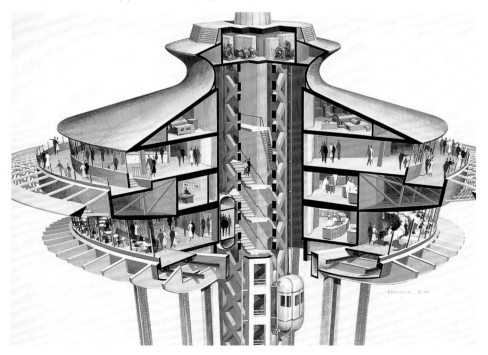

The million-dollar restaurant, called Top of the Needle, Inc., was run by a wholly owned subsidiary of Western International Hotels. Harry Mullikin—who was selected as project manager to oversee design, furnishing, and selection and training of the crew—ultimately became chief executive officer of Westin Hotels.

The outer rim of the revolving restaurant made a 360-degree turn every 60 minutes, giving visitors spectacular views of the Cascades, with the 10,775-foot snow-capped Mount Baker to the north, then craggy Glacier Peak and the 14,411-foot Mount Rainier, followed by the sight of Puget Sound and, on a clear day, Mount Adams and Mount St. Helens. Then came a view of downtown Seattle and a look across Puget Sound to the Olympics, and north toward the Strait of Juan de Fuca.

Mullikin recounted solutions to logistical problems that came with a revolving restaurant. "We hadn't thought about the fact that they [servers] were not going to be able to find the closest kitchen entrance. I sent someone down to the dime store to buy some colored tape." The tape was used to indicate the halfway point between the two kitchen doors.

The Graham-designed restaurant turntable was tested, including coffee service aboard, at Western Gear Corp. in Everett before it was disassembled and transported to the Needle.

Following page: Top house construction in early 1962.

TONIGHT IN THE SPACE NEEDLE...

It's a suspended-in-space kind of a place.
Like nothing on Earth, a laughter and mirth.
Kind of a place.
It's a OOO-feet-tall feeling for all; a
Roses-and-wine, where epicures dine
Kind of a place.
A sprawl-in, sit-tall-in kind of a place.

A quiet lair, a want-to-be-there, a welcome face
Kind of a place.
It's a tall-one-all-tinkly, a smile all wrinkly.
It's a wonderful food, wonderful mood,
Kind of a place.
It's excitement and fun, adventure begun, a
Candlelight and spotlight
Kind of a place.

WESTERN INTERNATIONAL HOTELS

"When the waitress went into the kitchen, she would come back out with no idea where her table had gone." To assist servers, the dining area was divided into four sections, each subtly color-coded.

"Guests had the same problem. They would get up to go to the restroom, but when they came back, they couldn't find their tables," mused Mullikin.

Mullikin's concern about recovering the company's investment was soon quelled. The restaurant operation paid for itself in three months. No one was happier than Eddie Carlson, who dined on top in the restaurant at a banquet the night before the Fair opened. Among the people in his party were Mr. and Mrs. Moffett, who had joined Carlson and his wife, Nell, at the Stuttgart Tower, as well as Margot Colden, who had first suggested that they all have dinner at the Stuttgart Tower that night just three years earlier.

The Symbol of the Fair

The Space Needle sold the Fair to the world. Public relations expert Jay Rockey was able to get two cover stories in *Life* magazine, which was the most important media outlet of its day.

"Without the Space Needle, a *Life* cover would have been a very, very tough sell," said Rockey.

Some 2.3 million people rode up the Space Needle during the World's Fair, which attracted 9,634,601 people. "The Fair made Seattle an important city and enabled Seattle to become known around the world much more than it had been," said Rockey. "Any city that's going to be a major city has got to have a symbol. The Space Needle became the symbol and it enabled Seattle to become a truly world-class city."

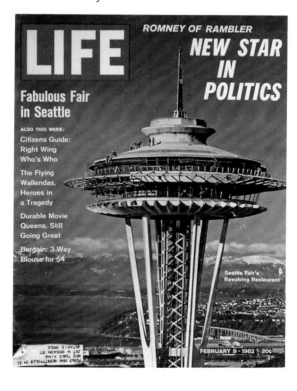

Two 1962 *Life* magazine covers ensured an audience of millions.

The Long-Term View

Ever since it became the focal point of the World's Fair, the Space Needle has sewn itself into the hearts of Seattleites, who closely follow the fortunes of their favorite building. Anything that affects the Space Needle affects Seattle.

On April 29, 1965, Seattle was shaken by an earthquake that measured between 6.5 and 7.0 on the Richter scale. While the Needle swayed a bit and was closed that day for safety precautions, it stood tall. Listeners of the KING-AM radio station were assured that all was well by breathless disc jockey Frosty Fowler, who regularly broadcast his morning show from a booth atop the Needle.

While people around the world immediately began identifying Seattle with the Space Needle, it took a little time for some Seattleites to adopt it as the symbol of their city. When the Seattle First National Bank Building (now Bank of America) became the tallest structure on the West Coast in 1969, the tall, dark edifice was referred to by locals as "the box the Space Needle came in."

In the early 1980s, a part of the citizenry objected to the proposal to build a restaurant, cocktail lounge, and meeting rooms at the 100-foot level of the Needle. There were outcries at public hearings, negative Seattle Council votes, and court decisions; there were letters to the editor, cartoons, and editorials in the local newspapers. Critics were unswayed by the argument that the original design provided for two other observation platforms, one at the 100-foot level and one at the 300-foot level, although they were not built.

By this time, there were two remaining owners of the original five that made up Pentagram: Howard S. Wright and Jack Graham. Wright was firmly committed to seeing the 100-foot level built, and having Jack Graham design it. Eventually, the State Court of Appeals gave the go-ahead, and the addition was built.

Opposite: The most notable addition to the original Space Needle, the Pavilion, was completed in 2000. Shown is Pavilion construction in 1999.

When the 100-foot level controversy was taking place, Eddie Carlson got a kick out of it, recalled his daughter, Jane Carlson Williams. "He loved the fact that the citizens had embraced it as our city's symbol, and were saying, 'How dare you change it?' That was very satisfying to him." It was clear that by this time, the community thought of the Space Needle as an important part of their city.

Around that same time, the Space Needle Corporation took over the operation of the restaurant from Westin Hotels at the end of a 20-year lease agreement and developed plans for its refurbishing. The ensuing sale of the original fixtures and furnishings was described by veteran auctioneer James G. Murphy as "the biggest restaurant auction in the history of Seattle—and also the most scenic." More than 300 people participated in the daylong bidding on a total of 1,600 lots of various items, including crystal wine glasses, glass bowls, and ashtrays. Today, the relics are considered collector's items and sell for many times the value established at the time of the auction.

During the 1980s, the remodeling of the restaurant, the renovation of the top house, and the 100-foot level addition cost five million dollars—which was about what it cost to build the original structure.

The Space Needle restaurant is shown after renovation in 1985.

The SkyLine Level, which houses a kitchen and banquet facilities, was completed in 1982.

SkyCity, the Needle's current revolving restaurant, was redesigned, renamed, and reopened in 2000.

Pride in Ownership

In 1976, three of the original five investors, Bagley Wright, D. E. "Ned" Skinner, and Norton Clapp, sold their interests in the Pentagram Corporation, which owned the Needle and, by then, the Bank of California building, to Howard S. Wright and Jack Graham. During the early eighties, Wright and Graham divided the Pentagram properties, with Graham getting the bank building and Wright the Space Needle.

Second-generation owner and Space Needle Corporation Chairman Jeffrey Wright saw that "for years the Space Needle was a challenge . . . it wasn't a positive operation. But my father had this burning quest to maintain his ownership of it."

Becoming the sole owner of the Space Needle was a source of personal pleasure and civic pride to Howard S. Wright, whose firm had overseen the construction of the Space Needle back in those busy, intense days of 1961-62. Wright even had business cards printed with his name on the front and a free ticket for admission to the Space Needle on the back. He gave those cards to everyone he met, and some of them still show up at the ticket window today!

"My father would be seated next to some-body on an airplane, and within 10 minutes, that person would know that my father built and owned the Space Needle, and then he'd invite that person to come to the Space Needle for lunch," recalled Jeffrey Wright, who visited the construction site as a four-year-old. "When the structural steel was in the sky and the actual restaurant deck had been put on, I went up on a construction elevator with my father, holding on to his legs. I remember lying on my stomach, looking over the side, with my dad hanging on to me by my ankles."

Howard S. Wright could often be found at the Needle, talking and visiting with elevator operators, cooks, and visitors. It was clear to employees of the Needle that they were working for an owner who had a passion for it. Upon his death in 1996, a new generation of the Wright family took up the reins.

The view straight down from the partially constructed top house during construction in 1962.

Bellwether of the Community

Under the stewardship of the Wright family, the Space Needle has expanded its ties to the City of Seattle. "We want the Space Needle to be a bellwether of the community," said board member Stuart Rolfe. Beyond being the symbol of Seattle, the Needle is a reflection of and a forum for the community. For example, when the 1991 football team of the University of Washington won the National Championship, coach Don James was up on the roof of the Needle painting the Husky "W." The Needle often commemorates the accomplishments of the community.

In keeping with community spirit, the Space Needle was decorated in recognition of the 1991 University of Washington Huskies' National Football Championship.

In 1992, a new tradition began—New Year's Eve fireworks at the Space Needle, which "caught the imagination of locals and people outside of Seattle and has helped us become the Times Square of the West," said Jeffrey Wright. "There's something unique about seeing fireworks go off of a 605-foot structure. This generation of my family enjoys giving that to the community." The production, sponsored by the Space Needle, is a highlight of the New Year's Eve "tour" that has become possible with modern technology, seen on television by millions of celebrants around the world.

Investment in the Future

By the late eighties, the Space Needle was in
need of some updating. The lack of parking
and the inadequacy of the flat-roofed entrance
to the elevators—put up as a "temporary"
shelter for visitors in 1965—sparked what
would become a 15-year process of revitalizing
and renovating the symbol of Seattle.

During the Fair, guests had to endure a long
line exposed to the elements to get to the
elevators. Hotelier Mullikin found to his
surprise that the people who waited in line for
hours and hours were nice. "One time when
I was working the line, I told people, 'It's 2:00
and there are so many people ahead of you
you're not going to get in in time for lunch.'
They'd say, 'What time does dinner start?'
When I told them 5:00, they would say, 'Okay,
we'll wait for dinner.'" At that time, a few
hard, fiberglass chairs at the front of the line
were the only source of comfort. All this
changed in the summer of 2000.

In conjunction with the City of Seattle, the
Seattle Center, and the Landmarks Preservation
Board, a new entrance, turn-around, fountain,
and base-level pavilion were created by
landscape and architectural design groups,
including Callison Architecture, Inc., which
designed the Pavilion.

The SpaceBase gift
shop was opened
in Summer 2000.

Painting the Space Needle is a costly and elaborate task that has been completed four times since its original "Astronaut White" legs were coated in 1962.

The design of the Pavilion arose out of ideas in the original sketches and illustrations for Century 21 (see the illustration on page 38). The spiraling glass pavilion allowed for a comfortable and roomy arrival space, while keeping the massive legs of the Needle clear of obstruction.

At the same time, the huge task of stripping, priming, and repainting the entire structure was under way. This process, including the minute inspection and ultrasound testing of the beams and bolts, cost almost as much as the building of the original Needle. The investment was worth it, though, noted the Director of Facilities, Rick Harris. "The structure is a grade and size of steel that you just don't see anymore."

A number of interesting issues arose during the renovation project. For example, it was known that because of the size of the disk-like top house, the Space Needle actually extended out beyond the property line of the 120-by-120-foot lot. Easements were procured to access this space, 550 feet above the property line.

The Pavilion Level redevelopment coincided with the relocation of the front entrance from Thomas Street off Fifth Avenue to Broad Street, where a circular valet and drop-off area around the new Howard S. Wright Memorial Fountain reflects the top house's "flying saucer" design.

Following page: The principal changes to the Space Needle since 1962 include the SkyLine Level, the Pavilion, the circular drive entrance, and the Howard S. Wright Memorial Fountain.

In 2001, as part of a promotional campaign, the daredevil acrobats of Planet Ringula performed outside the Observation Deck, giving visitors both unparalleled views and unexpected entertainment.

Opposite: Cirque du Soleil performed during the 2000 grand reopening ceremony at the Space Needle.

"The mark of this generation of owners is the Pavilion Level, which is a dynamic space," said Jeffrey Wright. "The Space Needle is the shoulder of the city to the north. We want the ground level to be equally dynamic for both vehicles and pedestrians."

Live the View

Designed with a concept theme of "Live the View," the project included construction of the two-story glass Pavilion Level, which contains the SpaceBase retail store, and the renovation of the restaurant, renamed SkyCity at the Needle.

The Space Needle attracts over 1.2 million visitors each year. The restaurant is one of the busiest in the country, with 300,000 annual out-of-city visitors and residents alike who thrill at the opportunity to dine atop the Needle and view the Seattle skyline, which has changed spectacularly since 1962.

In an effort to make the Space Needle more interactive, the Observation Deck was redesigned. "The O Deck is all about the view,"

The Observation Deck offers a 360-degree view.

noted Dean Nelson, President of the Space Needle Corporation. "The activities we have here have to complement the view; they are things you can only experience up here."

To celebrate the grand re-opening, acrobats of the famed Cirque du Soleil performed death-defying stunts on the Needle's Halo high above the ground. From the new interactive stations positioned around the Observation Deck to the live acrobatic performances out on the rim of the Halo, the unequaled panoramic view is not just the backdrop, but the main event on O Deck. With the addition of the SkyCafe coffee and food bar, one can Live the View in true Seattle style.

The Space Needle and its Legacy Lights in 2001.

Looking to the Future

To the current ownership, the responsibility of owning the Space Needle, a universally recognized icon, is one they take seriously.

"We feel fortunate to be the custodians of this great symbol of the city," said Jeffrey Wright. "Our stewardship is considered in our thinking. When we make a decision, we consider the financial and social implications. Will it enhance the importance of the Space Needle to the city? We want that to be our primary focus both for Seattle residents and for visitors. If you live in Seattle, we want you to say, 'This is *my* Space Needle.'"

Here is everything you ever wanted to know about the Space Needle.

The Space Needle's Spaces

In 2002, the Space Needle's guest facilities included the Pavilion at ground level, SkyLine banquet facility on the 100-foot level, SkyCity Restaurant at the 500-foot (152 meters) level, and the Observation Deck at 520 feet (158.5 meters).

The Needle's original cost was $4.5 million.

The June 2000 Pavilion Level, SkyCity Restaurant, and Observation Deck remodel cost was $21 million.

From design approval on March 8, 1961, to completion it took 407 days.

The Space Needle opened on April 21, 1962.

The lot is only 120 feet by 120 feet, but the Halo has a diameter of 138 feet.

The height from the ground to the aircraft warning beacon is 605 feet (184 meters).

At the time of its completion, the Space Needle was the tallest building west of the Mississippi River.

On April 21, 1999, the city's Landmarks Preservation Board named the Space Needle an official City of Seattle Landmark.

The Space Needle is designed to twist rather than lean in a high wind. The twisting actually takes place at the narrowest section of the tower.

The Space Needle sways approximately 1 inch for every 10 mph of wind.

The Space Needle was designed to withstand 150-mph winds.

Opposite: Space Needle, 2002.

Facts & Figures

The strongest wind recorded at the top of the Needle was over 90 mph. The Space Needle endures intermittent winds of 75-85 mph every year and has never suffered any damage. Engineers provided strength 50 percent above the Seattle Building Code provision for 100-mph winds.

On a hot day, the Needle expands about 1 inch.

The base is 125.25 feet above sea level.

Steel and concrete, May 1961.

The center of gravity is about 5 feet above ground level. The Space Needle weighs 9,550 tons: 3,700 tons of structure on a 5,850-ton foundation.

The Space Needle is fastened to its foundation with 72 bolts, each 32 feet long and 4 inches in diameter.

It took 467 truckloads of concrete (2,800 cubic yards) to complete the foundation.

The foundation is reinforced with 250 tons of rebar steel.

The Space Needle's original colors were "Astronaut White" for the legs, "Orbital Olive" for the core, "Re-entry Red" for the halo, and "Galaxy Gold" for the sunburst and pagoda roof.

The Needle has been painted four times since 1962.

It takes nearly 2,000 gallons of paint to coat the Needle.

Elevator Service

The last elevator car arrived the day before the Fair opened.

Two of the elevators are high speed and can travel at a rate of 10 mph, or 800 feet per minute. The third and slower (400 feet per minute) elevator is for freight.

Actual travel time for the passenger elevators at 10 mph, from the ground level to the top house, is 43 seconds.

When winds around the Needle reach high speeds, the traveling speed of the elevators is reduced to 5 mph for safety.

An early elevator-car design for the Space Needle.

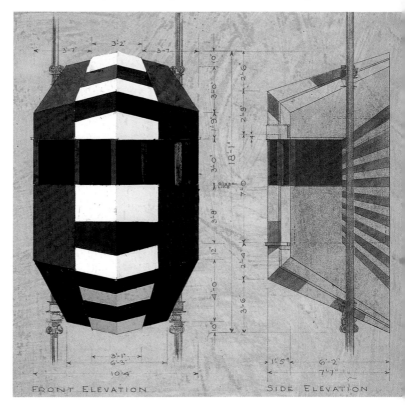

FRONT ELEVATION   SIDE ELEVATION

Each elevator is suspended on six cables, any one of which can hold the weight of the elevator and counterweight. A separate governor cable regulates the speed of the car.

Two electrical cables supply the power and controls for the elevators.

The three elevators were replaced in 1993 at a cost of $1.5 million.

Each elevator weighs about 14,000 pounds. The counterweight for each elevator weighs 15,800 pounds.

During the World's Fair, nearly 20,000 people a day rode the elevators. (The 20,000 mark was never quite attained, however, missing by fewer than 50 people one day.)

The Space Needle hosted over 2.3 million visitors during the Fair, when the wait for the elevator was up to three hours.

There are 848 steps from the bottom of the basement to the top of the Observation Deck. (There are 822 steps from the bottom of the basement to the SkyCity Restaurant.)

The Pavilion

The Pavilion was completed in 2000. It is the guest entrance for the Space Needle elevators and a space-age gift shop.

A typical line for the Space Needle elevator during the Fair.

The Space Needle
Pavilion, 2002.

More than 200 copyrights were granted for souvenir items during the World's Fair, and many have become valuable collectibles.

One of the best-sellers during the Fair was a Needle-shaped gold charm with a light in it, selling for about $75 in 1962. Another was a nine-inch-high chrome lighter in the shape of the Needle.

With 634 windows on its walls and 356 panes on the roof, the Pavilion covers roughly 23,000 square feet of area. The roof is about 55 percent glass. It measures 40 feet from floor to roof.

The capacity for the Pavilion, which includes the SkyCity and Observation Deck elevator waiting area and the SpaceBase gift shop, is 1,167 people.

The original elevator waiting area was a long line with little cover.

The SkyLine Level

The SkyLine Level was completed in 1982, and because of its elevation, it is often simply referred to as the "100-foot level."

A viewing platform at 100 feet was part of the Space Needle's original design, but it was not added until 1982.

There are two banquet rooms in the SkyLine Level that can accommodate groups of 20-350 guests.

84

SkyCity Restaurant

SkyCity seats 250 people.

The restaurant is perched more than 500 feet above the Seattle Center.

The diameter of the SkyCity Restaurant is 94.5 feet.

SkyCity is the third 500-foot restaurant at the Space Needle. The original restaurant was operated for 20 years by Westin Hotels.

In 1966, the restaurant was renovated and renamed "Eye of the Needle." In 1982, it was divided into two areas: the Space Needle Restaurant and the Emerald Suite Lounge.

The seating area of the restaurant rotates, while the kitchen remains stationary.

The turntable makes a full revolution approximately every hour.

The revolving restaurant design was a patented system created by Space Needle architect Jack Graham.

Ground-level reception area for the Space Needle's SkyCity Restaurant.

The Space Needle's revolving restaurant was the second in the world and was based on the revolving restaurant that Graham had just designed for the Ala Moana Shopping Center in Honolulu. There are now hundreds of turntables throughout the world.

The original restaurant turntable revolved on a track-and-wheel system that weighed roughly 125 tons.

The turntable is driven by a 1.5-horsepower electric motor.

The original restaurant turntable was replaced in 1985. In 2002, the tracks and wheels were upgraded to include technical advances for a smooth ride.

There are 48 windows in the restaurant. One opens to permit window-washer access.

An overhead rail outside the restaurant windows secures a platform for one of the world's most spectacular window-washing jobs.

The Observation Deck

There are several high-powered telescopes on the Observation Deck.

The widest part of the top house, the Halo below the Observation Deck, is 138 feet across.

The Seattle skyline and Elliott Bay as seen from the roof of the Space Needle in 2002.

Renovated in 2001, the Observation Deck provides viewers and photographers an unmatched 360-degree view of the Cascade Mountain range to the east, Mount Rainier and the Seattle skyline to the south,

Elliott Bay and the Olympic Mountains to the west, and Lake Union and Mount Baker to the north.

The Observation Deck interior renovation added a coffee and snack shop (SkyCafe), interactive guides to the view, and a visual history of the Space Needle.

Space Needle
Observation Deck,
2001.

Lore and Legend

The first Space Needle Manager, Hoge Sullivan, had acrophobia, a fear of heights.

After the Fair, the city of Fife, Washington, offered $1 million to move the Space Needle to its downtown.

The Committee Hoping for Extra-Terrestrial Encounters to Save the Earth (CHEESE) claims to have plans from the 1962 World's Fair that show the Space Needle was constructed to send transmissions to advanced beings in other solar systems.

During the Fair, private planes that flew near the Needle were reported to the authorities only if they were so close that their tail-numbers could be read.

There have been six parachute jumps from the Needle; two were unauthorized, and the other four were part of a promotion.

As an April Fool's joke, a local television station aired a phony report that the Space Needle had fallen over. Emergency phone lines were swamped with calls. The Space Needle received more than 700 calls, even though there was a flashing alert during the entire report telling the audience that it was a joke. One Spokane man even jumped in his car and began driving to Seattle because his daughter worked at the Space Needle.

The Space Needle "moved" 312 feet southwest in June 1987. That year, the National Oceanic and Atmospheric Administration (NOAA) began a 10-year project to more accurately map the Earth using satellite technology. Part of their plan was to use prominent structures such as the Space Needle as landmarks for the new maps. When the Space Needle's position was plotted using the extremely accurate information generated by the satellites high above the Earth, it was determined that the old maps were off by 312 feet. Therefore, the Space Needle appears to have moved on the new maps.

A cold snap in December 1968 froze pipes at 10 degrees below zero Fahrenheit, closing the top house for five days. More insulation was added.

In 1974, as a radio personality promotion, a small apartment and broadcast booth were constructed for a disc jockey. The apartment was 1,200 square feet, 18 percent of the Observation Deck, and cost $50,000.

Since its inception in 1992, the Space Needle's annual New Year's Eve celebration has grown to be the West Coast's premier New Year's Eve event.

In May 1996, the Space Needle welcomed the Olympic Torch Relay with a special fireworks show as it passed through Seattle on its way to Atlanta for the Summer Games. The torch came through again in 2002 for the Winter Olympics in Salt Lake City.

Project Bandaloop
performs on the
vertical stage of the
Space Needle.

Following page:
The Space Needle
and the city
skyline from Queen
Anne Hill.

Photo Credits

Front

Introduction

One

Two

Index

Further Reading

Carlson, Edward E.
Recollections of a Lucky Fellow
Seattle: 1989.

Doherty, Craig A. and Katherine M.
The Seattle Space Needle
Woodbridge, CT: Blackbirch Press, 1997.

Duncan, Don
Meet Me at the Center: The Story of Seattle Center . . .
Seattle: Seattle Center Foundation, 1992.

Mansfield, Harold, and George Gulacsik
Space Needle USA
Seattle: The Craftsman Press, 1962

Mansfield, Harold
Space Needle; Seattle's Landmark: How It Happened
Edmonds, WA: Creative Communications Publishing, 1986.

Morgan, Murray Cromwell
Century 21: The Story of the Seattle World's Fair, 1962
Seattle: Acme Press, distributed by University of Washington Press, 1963.

The Space Needle Story
Seattle: Space Needle Corporation, 1992 (Videotape).